Dinkum Complete Guide

Guido Harber

ii

ISBN: 979-8-3605-9228-0

CONTENTS

Dinkum is a create your own island game where you can farm plants, hunt animals, explore dangerous mines and build up your own town. The game allows you to play it however you like; if you prefer to fish all day or hunt vicious animals, that's up to you! Dinkum is a popular farming simulator also, with players able to create their own crop fields to harvest the latest plants.

The character's desire to leave behind a place with no passion and fulfilment takes you to a location where you have to start off by building tents and entertaining visitors. Slowly, you'll progress towards building a town and having a permanent residence for people to settle down in.

TIPS FOR BEGINNER

Don't Be Afraid To Explore

The world of Dinkum is vast, and the amount of things players can discover on the island even more so. While it can be somewhat nerve-wracking to wander far from one's settlement, especially early on when supplies and tools are low, players shouldn't be afraid to wander all around the island.

Plenty of ores, wood, fish, and bugs are unique to specific biomes, and the more the player explores, the more they'll be rewarded, especially early on. So long as the player stays alert (and even if they don't), the reward far outweighs the risk.

Pay Attention To The Wildlife

Wildlife in Dinkum can be found everywhere players turn. Whether they're diggos, jackaroos, or crocos, every creature in Dinkum has something to offer, and ways they'll interact with other animals around them. The behavior of carnivores in particular will prove indispensable to early-game players who are lacking proper weapons.

Should a player need meat during their exploration, following a pack of diggos is bound to lead them to some leftover meat from their jackaroo hunts, which players can take without needing to enter combat at all.

Collect As Many Materials As Possible

Early in Dinkum, the most reliable ways to progress are through earning Dinks, which can be used to pay off debts and buy tools, and Permit Points, which pay for deeds and licenses. In both cases, the best way to earn them, especially early on, is by collecting anything and everything players can get their hands on.

Not only can players earn Dinks by selling what they collect to John, but the act of collecting, gathering, and selling items will progress players' milestone goals, earning them a lot of Permit Points as well.

Stamina Refills Over Time

One thing players need to keep an eye on as they explore is their stamina bar. Stamina is needed for most things players can do during the day, including mining, combat, swimming, and catching things. Should the player start to tire out, eating food is a quick way to regain some energy.

However, players should still pace themselves, and they can only eat three things at a time before they'll have to wait until they're hungry again. Luckily, players can regain energy simply by taking a break and waiting for the bar to refill.

Talk To Residents Every Day

Residents provide more to the player than what's in their job descriptions. Every day, players can chat to learn more about the characters' lives and what brought them to the island, as well as offer to help them out with whatever they need.

Every resident will usually have a request the player can fulfill by the end of the day, after which they'll be rewarded with Dinks, items, or even blueprints. For players just starting their town, the recipes and resources they exchange with residents goes a long way into developing their new home, as well as building relationships with their neighbors.

Be Prepared: Carry A Weapon

It should come as no surprise that the world of Dinkum is a wild one. Whether players are exploring the mines, traversing the land, or swimming through the rivers of their island, they're bound to encounter danger on their adventures. As a result, acquiring a hunting license early on goes a long way into keeping players safe.

Beyond just that, however, is the rewards that each creature has to offer when they're bested in combat. The more dangerous the animal, the better the rewards compared to less deadly animals like diggos and jackaroos, and players can reap the rewards of better food and crafting materials.

Keep A Stash Of Supplies

Selling as many resources as possible early on is not only easy, but provides an immediate reward in the form of Dinks for the player. However, as soon as the player has the means to create crates, they should start saving resources as well, even (and especially) if their use isn't readily apparent.

Things like woods, ores, and even the strange metal scraps players find from oil drums can turn out to be vital for later crafting recipes and objectives. When in doubt, holding onto even a handful of mystery items can pay off later, whether it's for construction, crafting, or even cooking.

Catch Every Bug And Fish In Sight

Bug catching and fishing are going to be one of the most reliable and consistent moneymakers players can turn to in Dinkum. In addition to an easy source of Permit Points as players catch whichever bugs and fish they come across, they also sell surprisingly high at the general store.

Moreover, the different types of fish and bugs spawn in different areas, and learning these early on will prove helpful when the time comes to catch specific bugs and fish for the museum later, which rewards players with Permit Points for every new donation.

Be Careful At Night

The sun sets early and quickly in Dinkum, and players will have to plan their days around it. For the most part, the night is harmless. Players can navigate the dark or carry a torch, find and catch night-specific creatures like fireflies, and talk to their neighbors as they wrap up the day.

However, if players are wandering far from their town, they should keep an eye out, as some nocturnal creatures are more dangerous than others. If players don't have a means of protection, they should be ready to run should they encounter any bush devils while they're out exploring.

Level Up Skills Early

Gathering resources early on is a good idea anyway, especially with so many things to craft and build to establish the town. However, logging and mining in particular are important skills to level up early on, as reaching level 10 will unlock a newer license that lets players craft new and improved tools.

Not only will these new tools last longer and save players time and money early on, but they will also allow players to gather resources the beginner tools couldn't break, which will be required for other skills, licenses, and crafting recipes.

WALKTHROUGH

NEW GAME - PART 1

Welcome to the Dinkum Walkthrough and Game Guide; we'll be following the Dinkum main scenario tasks for this game guide- but the game never really ends! There's always more farming to be done, more hunting to be had and lots of cool adventures awaiting for you!

- Dinkum New Game

- The South

- Dinkum Island - Base Tent

- Dinkum User Interface

- Island Travelers

- Adventure Journal

- Camp Fire and Fruit

Whilst the game is still in Early Access at the start of writing this Dinkum Walkthrough, we'll go back and rewrite anything if it becomes outdated. Just let us know in the comments!

For now, get comfortable and prepare to dive into your own unique world...

Dinkum New Game

You can create as many islands as you like; each New Game starts out the same with you starting with nothing but a blank canvas with the hopes one day turning your island into a sprawling village.

The game works on a night/day system, where each time you go to bed, your progress is saved and all the tasks you did that day are then translated into XP to level up your skills and progression.

There is plenty to do in Dinkum, so starting a new game can be a little overwhelming at first. But this walkthrough should hand-hold you until you get comfortable with the mechanics and want to go off and explore on your own.

Before you start the game, you get to customize your character! Don't spend too long worrying about your outfit, as you'll have plenty of new items to find once you're on your island.

Give your character a name and name your Island.

The South

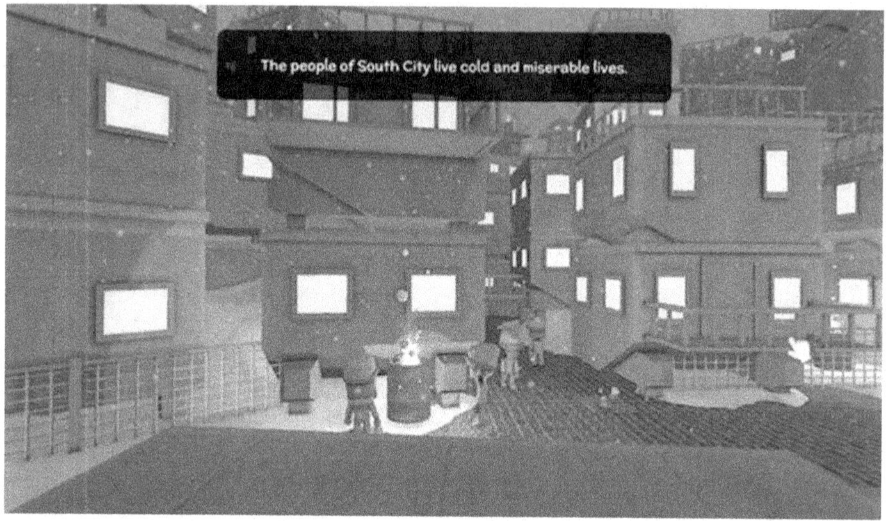

You begin your adventure in the depressing town of South City. There is no fun here, with it's bleak and grey colors.

But luckily for you, you see a notice looking for a "young go-getter" to help out the NPC Fletch on his old Island. This is your golden ticket out of here!

After meeting Fletch, you take off in an Airship and arrive at your

Island.

Dinkum Island - Base Tent

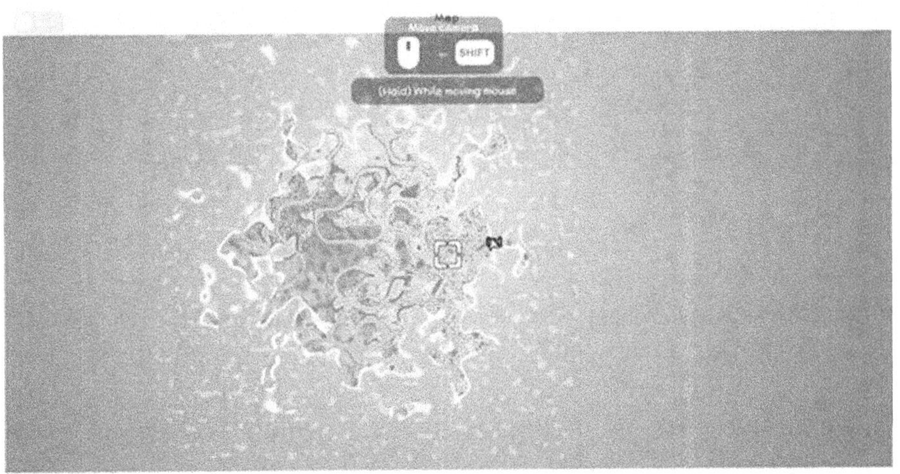

Your Island is generated uniquely for each New Game that you start. Your Island will have it's own unique rivers and islets, it's own areas that are full of palm trees and others which are barren deserts. Pretty cool eh?

Once you land, speak to Fletch and he will give you your Base Tent and Map.

Your first task is to setup the Base Tent. The Base Tent is where you'll get to speak to Fletch at the start of a new day for new tasks.

Choosing your Base Tent location doesn't matter too much, but we do recommend somewhere that is closer in the middle, with access to water (for farming). With your Base Tent being in the middle of the map, you'll have closer access to all the areas around you.

Press M to take a look at your Island. You can put down markers to help you navigate around; your Base Tent will always show up on the map.

TIP: As you move around the map looking for the perfect spot, start foraging items you find. You'll notice lots of trees full of fruit, bushes on the ground and shells on the beach. All of this stuff you can sell later for money, as well as leveling up your Foraging Skill.

Once you've set up the Base Tent, Fletch will talk to you again. Fletch will give you your very own Tent that you can use as your own home until you get something a little more permanent.

You'll want to keep your own Tent nearby, so you don't have to do a lot of traveling when you want to access it. Right next to the Base Tent works fine!

Once you've placed your own Tent, head inside Base Tent and talk to Fletch.

Dinkum User Interface

Now is a good time to break down the Dinkum User Interface.

Date and Time

Your Health and Stamina Bars. Health goes down when you're attacked by animals; Stamina goes down when you perform actions like mining, fishing and swimming.

Current Tasks; you can pin tasks to this menu from your Adventure Journal

1. Mini Map

2. Your clothes that you're currently wearing

3. Your Storage Slots

4. Your Toolbar; items in the Toolbar can be used by your character when selected.

5. Your Daily Milestone Tasks

Island Travelers

Throughout your time on your Island, you'll get visitors.

Each visitor can offer you something unique in exchange for money or items and you can also befriend them by performing quests and buying their goods. Do it enough, and they'll want to stay on your island permanently.

Fletch mentions that Traveling Trader John is going to visit soon.

Fletch hands you the Visiting Site Deed, which is an area that you should setup near the Base Tent. This is where all your visitors will arrive at, allowing you to interact with them- so you want to keep it close to your own setup.

Adventure Journal

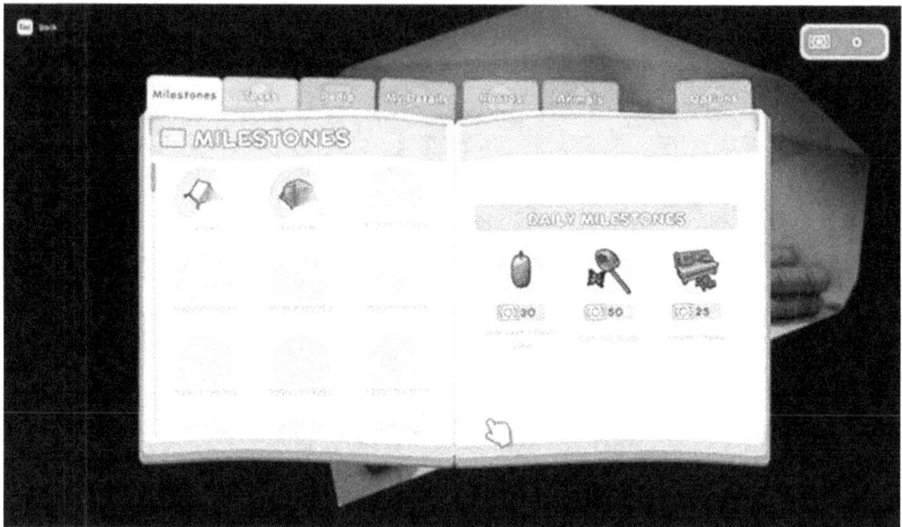

Once setup, head back inside the Base Tent and speak to Fletch. He will give you your Adventure Journal- this allows you to keep track of your Island's Progress, including any Tasks you're currently on.

You'll also get introduced to a new currency called Permit Points. You can earn these by completing Milestones and Daily Milestones, all viewable within the Adventure Journal.

There are lots of different Milestones to complete and it's best to dabble in a bit of everything at the beginning to start racking up the Permit Points.

Daily Milestones refresh each day; some Daily Milestones you won't be able to complete until you unlock various aspects of your Island.

Permit Points are incredibly important and you'll be using them to upgrade your skills, unlock new ones and upgrade your Island's facilities.

Camp Fire and Fruit

Next Fletch asks you to find something to eat.

You can find all sorts of eatables on your Island, but perhaps the easiest is to find Fruit from a Bush Lime. These are found in areas Bushland and are very common.

Depending on where your put your Base Tent, you might also find Strawberries and Bananas and a whole other host of fruit!

You might also get lucky and find some Meat on the ground. Meat comes from animals on your Island, but since you don't have any weapons yet you can't hunt. However, sometimes the animals attack each other and drop meat for you!

Once you've found something, head back to Fletch.

You'll be given the Camp Fire recipe, which allows you to craft a Camp Fire at the Crafting Table in the Base Tent.

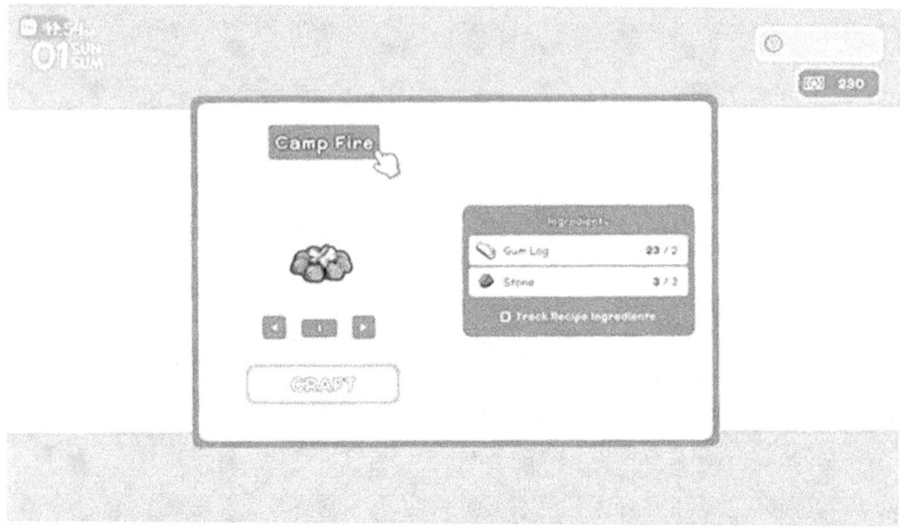

To craft a Camp Fire, you'll need 3 Stone and 2 Gum Log. Luckily, Fletch gives you 3 Stone automatically, so all you need to do is forage some Gum Log. These are in abundance everywhere on your Island, so hopefully you've been picking them up as you scouted for Fruit.

Head over to the Crafting Table in the Base Tent and craft a Camp Fire.

TIP: A Camp Fire can be used to Cook food. Cooked food, when eaten, will regenerate your health and stamina bars more than uncooked food. You can cook Meat and those Bush Limes.

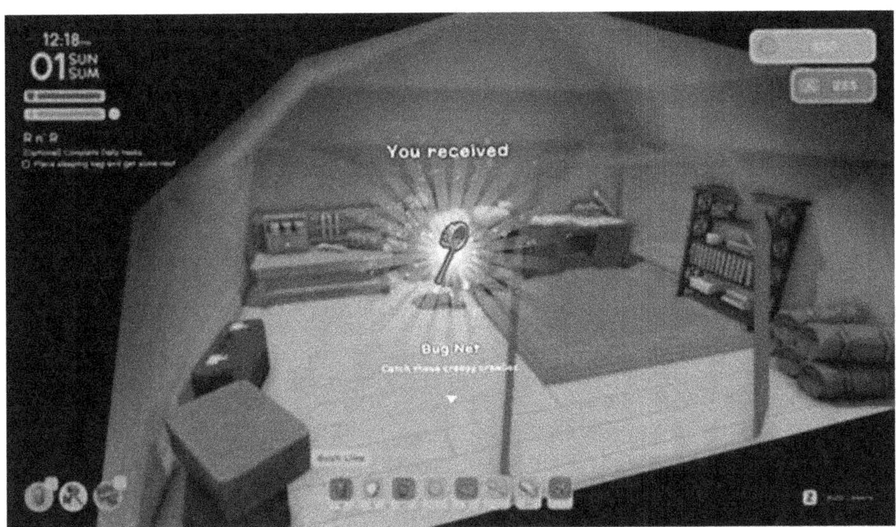

Once crafted, speak to Fletch again and this time he will give you a Bug Net and a Sleeping Bag.

A Bug net can be used to capture bugs on the Island. You'll be able to sell these Bugs later, so if you see any, make sure to capture them!

The Sleeping Bag item can be put down anywhere on your Island (inside and out!) and allows you to start the next day.

Your next tasks won't become available until the new day starts, so if you're done with all your foraging and using the Camp Fire, put out your Sleeping Bag and get some zzzs.

JOHN'S GOODS - PART 2

In this part of the Dinkum Walkthrough we accommodate Traveling Trader John to our Island. You'll be getting visitors to your Island quite often, and John is the first one that you have to convince to stay.

- An Introduction To Dinkum Licences

- Early Money In Dinkum

- Smelting Ore

- Getting John To Stay

- John's Permanent Residential Building

Whenever you start a new day, there is a chance you'll get a new visitor to your Island. You'll know when someone has arrived because a short cutscene plays out to alert you of it.

They are always in the Visiting Site Tent and you can go meet them to buy goods, do tasks and chat with them.

Traveling Trader John is the default first Island visitor and there are a series of un-skippable tasks you need to complete to get him to stay.

An Introduction To Dinkum Licences

Go and speak to Fletch to start the next Task in the Base Tent.

He will introduce you to Dinkum Licences, which you need to be able to perform certain actions. They cost Permit Points, and at this stage you might not have acquired too many.

We recommend acquiring the Mining Licence first, as it will help with upcoming tasks.

Once you have your new Licence, speak to Fletch again and he tells you about the Table Saw item that John is selling in his shop. He gives you half the money (2,500 Dinks!) for it, so you need to come up with the rest.

Early Money In Dinkum

Traveling Trader John will buy everything you have. Any items you find on the floor, mine, harvest or cook, John will buy! You need a total of 5,200 Dinks to buy a Table Saw.

We recommend buying a Pickaxe so you can also start mining for 1,200 Dinks.

One of the best ways to start earning Dinks is to go foraging early on. Foraging doesn't consume any Stamina points, so you're free to do it for as long as possible. Just be wary of swimming- as that does consume points.

Below is a table of easy-to-find items that you can sell for some Dinks.

Item	Find	Sells For

Yellow Wattle Flower	Obtain 2-3 from Wattle Bushes found all over your Island.	145 Dinks
Bush Lime	Obtain 2-3 from Bush Lime Trees found all over your Island.	90 Dinks
Gum Log	Found on the floor all over the Island Also comes from Gum Trees when you chop them down with an Axe.	100 Dinks
Ulysses Butterfly	Kind of rare compared to the others, but sell for a decent amount.	660 Dinks

Once you have earned 5,200 Dinks, go and purchase the Table Saw from Traveling Trader John.

Smelting Ore

After purchasing the Table Saw, go and talk to Fletch to start the next Task when you're ready. In order to start building permanent buildings on the Island, you're going to need a furnace to smelt ore.

Fletch asks you to bring him the following items:

1x Camp Fire

3x Stone

10x Tin Ore

The Camp Fire you already have; however you can Craft another for 2x Gum Log and 3x Stone, which should be pretty easy to do now that you have a Pickaxe. Stone comes from regular rocks around your Island.

In order to get Tin Ore, you're going to need a Pickaxe and Mining Licence (if you haven't purchased one already) and find Tin Ore Rocks. These can be pretty difficult to find when you're new to the game, so keep your eye out for them.

Tin Ore Rocks can drop up to 3 Tin Ore at a time, so you're going to need to find around 4 Tine Ore Rocks.

We had lots of success finding Tin Ore in Bushlands but you can find them pretty much anywhere.

Once you have all the materials, speak to Fletch and he will give you a Crude Furnace Recipe. This will allow you to craft a Crude Furnace, which can turn your Ore into Bars.

Fletch wants you to bring a Tin Bar, so go and craft the Crude Furnace inside the Base Tent.

To craft a Tin Bar, pop the Crude Furnace on the ground and insert 4 Tin Ore to create a Tin Bar. It takes around a minute for the Tin Bar to form.

Once you've given Fletch the Tin Bar, he gives you two new recipes: Nails and Wooden Crate.

Wooden Crates are extremely useful as you can store all your items in them. Its a good idea to craft several of these if you get the chance.

Getting John To Stay

Fletch says the next task is to convince John to stay on your Island. In order to do this, you need to purchase goods from his store and also complete daily tasks for him.

You can only complete one daily task for John each day, so you'll need to start new days by using your Sleeping Bag. John only needs two Daily Tasks completed before he accepts to live on your Island.

To start a Daily Task with John, select the "I want to chat" dialogue option, and then the "Need Something?" option.

John can give you a variety of different tasks- some you won't be able to complete based on circumstances. You can always just start a new day if you cannot complete his task.

You can see your Friendship Level with John above his name. Each task will increase your Friendship Level with John by 25% of a heart. You only need 50% of a Heart for him to stay- so that's two Daily Tasks.

Now is a great time to start buying more Licences and Tools from John so you can perform more tasks when out in the wild.

John's Permanent Residential Building

Once you have completed two Daily Tasks for John and spent some money in his shop, talk to him and he will tell you he wants to stay on your Island permanently!

Go and talk to Fletch in the Base Tent. Select the option "Talk about the town..." and "Can I see those deeds?".

Here you can purchase the Shop Deed needed for John. It will put your Island in 75,000 Dinks of Debt- but don't worry about that for now.

Once purchased, go and place the Shop Deed outside for where you want John's shop to be.

You will then be required to deposit materials in order for the Shop to be constructed. Click on the Green Bin to see the items you need.

You'll need the following:

15x Gum Wood Plank

10x Palm Wood Plank

2x Tin Sheet

16x Nails

There are two new items here that you may not have seen before.

You can create planks of wood using your Table Saw.

Palm Wood Logs come from Palm Trees. Use your map to look for vegetation zones and find Palm Trees. Don't forget you'll need a Logging Licence and Basic Axe to chop these down.

Nails can be crafted using Tin Bars at the Crafting Table.

Tin Sheets can be gotten by using your Pickaxe on Metal Barrels. These Barrels are quite hard to find and pop up randomly all over your Island.

When you smash the Metal Barrels they drop all sorts of stuff, including the Tin Sheets.

Once you have all the materials, it will take 2 days for the Shop to be fully built.

Congratulations on setting up John's Permanent Residency! He has some new items for sale too!

PERMANENT RESIDENTS - PART 3

After setting up John's Goods Permanent Residency, we are now tasked with finding 5 Permanent Residents for our Island, in order to be officially recognized as an official settlement by The South.

- 5 Permanent Residents

- Island Visitors

- Dinkum - Money Making Methods

- Town Hall Available

- This task can be picked up by talking to Fletch.

The task only seems to become available after you have completed around 9 Days on your Island and got John's Goods store setup.

Keep talking to Fletch and this task will eventually pop-up. (Let us know in the comments if there is something specific to trigger this!)

Now that John is a permanent resident, he also has a few new items for sale. His shop opens at 8AM and closes at 5PM; outside of those hours John can be seen wondering around your Island.

Now is a good idea to get your Mining Level and Foraging Level up to 10 so you can unlock the new Mining and Logging Licenses to upgrade your Tools to Bronze.

5 Permanent Residents

The task for getting 5 Permanent Residents can be a little difficult at first, but once you understand the mechanics behind the NPCs it's actually pretty easy.

Every other day you'll get a new visitor to your Visiting Tent where they will sell you goods, buy items from you and allow you to do tasks for them to increase the Friendship Level.

In order to get them to stay, you need to do a few things. First, you will need to spend around 10-20K Dinks on items/services they have for sale.

Second, you'll need to increase the Friendship Level. Each NPC seems to have a different threshold for how many hearts you need in order to get them to join.

Once you complete those two tasks above, the NPC will then give you access to their Land Deed. You will need to talk to them in order for the Land Deed to become available; sometimes restarting the day and waiting for them to visit will trigger it.

You can view the Land Deeds by speaking to Fletch in the Base Tent.

In order to use a Land Deed, the Island must not be in debt. That means you're going to have to pay off the Dinks debt you incurred for John's Goods shop.

You can do this by going to the Base Tent and selecting the Donation Box behind Fletch to donate Dinks.

Once paid off, you can apply for the Land Deed of the NPC. You'll then need to place the land deed down on your Island, and find the required construction items in order for the permanent residency to be completed (takes around 2 days).

Luckily, you already have 2 Permanent Residents in John and Fletch, so you only need 3 more.

Island Visitors

Based on our play through, we have created this useful table to help you figure out how many hearts/tasks you need to complete in order for NPC to give you their Land Deed.

In order for certain visitors to come to your Island, you need to unlock their Level 1 Dinkum Licence first.

NPC	Friendship Level Required	Spending Requirement	Land Deed Debt	Building Type	Requirements

	Hearts				
 Rayne	♥♥ ♥♥ ♥	18,000 Dinks	200,000 Dinks	Plant Shop	Farming Licence
 Theodore	♥♥ ♥♥ ♥	0 Dinks	125,000 Dinks	Museum	Default
 Franklyn	♥♥ ♥♥ ♥	150,000 Dinks	250,000 Dinks	Crafting Lab	Default
 Clover	♥♥ ♥♥ ♥	10,000 Dinks	180,000 Dinks	Clothing Shop	Default

Sally	Currently cannot move in	305,000 Dinks	-	Salon	Have at least 4 residents moved in
Irwin	♥♥ ♥♥ ♥	25,000 Dinks	150,000	Animal Farm Shop	Handling Licence
Melvin	♥♥ ♥♥ ♥	800 Dinks	145,000	Furniture Shop	Upgrade base tent to a house

Remember, in order to apply for the Land Deed, you must first pay off any Island Debt, which means you're going to need to make a lot of Dinks!

Dinkum - Money Making Methods

Getting the 5/5 Residents on your Island is a costly task and you're going to need a lot of Dinks to do this. You can sell pretty much anything you farm, but there are certain items which are worth more than others. Here is a table of useful items you should look to acquire in order to make Dinks fast.

Shiny Discs

One quick way to make Dinks is to acquire Shiny Discs. You can then sell these items to Franklyn (when he comes to visit) for 8,800 Dinks each!

Shiny Discs can be found from Metal Barrels that pop-up all over your Island. You can find them much easier if you purchase the Metal Detector from John's Goods shop, as that will allow you to find them buried beneath you.

Old Contraption

Old Contraption is also a rare material item that can come from Metal Barrels. You can sell these to John at any time for a whopping 15,000

Dinks each!

Sell To John

As always, all items you farm you can sell to John for Dinks. Here are some of the better ones worth farming:

Item	Sell For	How To Find
Quartz Crystal	200 Dinks	Quartz Rocks
Cooked Meat	800 Dinks	Hunt animals and then cook Meat
Cooked Giant Drumstick	1,500 Dinks	Hunt Dodo Birds and then cook the Raw Giant Drumsticks

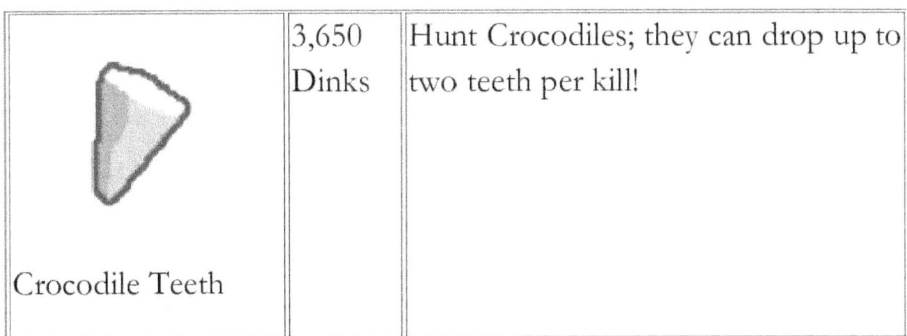	3,650 Dinks	Hunt Crocodiles; they can drop up to two teeth per kill!
Crocodile Teeth		

Town Hall Available

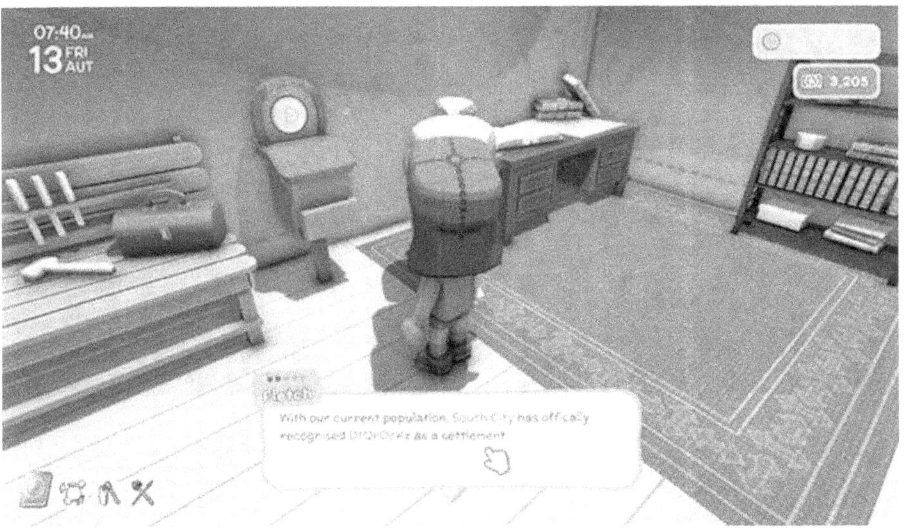

Once you have 5 Permanent Residents, speak to Fletch to complete the Task.

He now says you can upgrade the Base Tent into a Town Hall due to being recognized as an official settlement by The South. Hurrah!

You will need to find the materials to upgrade the Base Tent next. You can view them by clicking on the bin outside the tent.

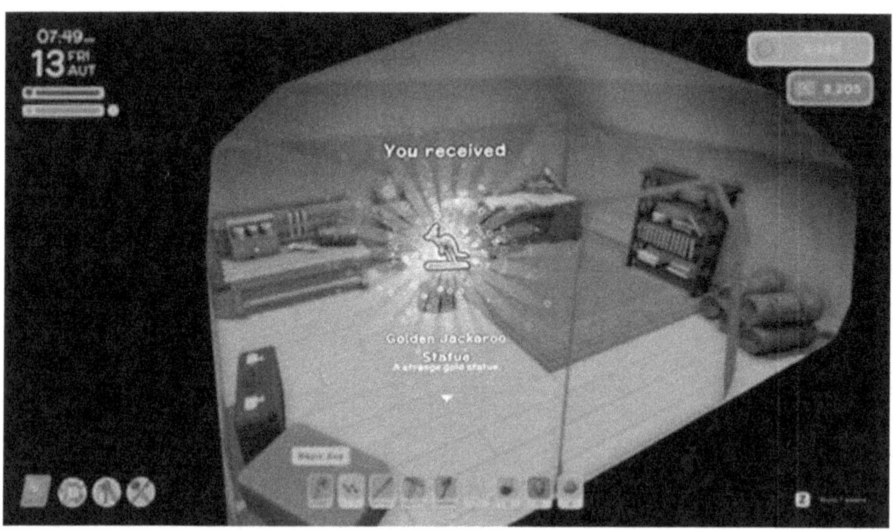

As a reward for getting 5 Permanent Residents, you also get a Golden Jackaroo Statue!

UPGRADING TOWN HALL - PART 4

After recruiting new residents to our Island, Fletch now allows us to upgrade our Base Tent to a Town Hall. In order to do this, we are going to need some new materials that require us to go into the Deep Mines.

As mentioned, in order to get the next task from Fletch, you need to have recruited 5 permanent residents to your Island. Afterwards, Fletch will let you upgrade the Base Tent to a Town Hall; a green bin will appear outside the Base Tent with the Construction Materials required.

In order to upgrade to a Town Hall, you're going to need the following:

● 15x Gum Wood Plank

● 15x Hard Wood Plank

● 4x Iron Bar

● 4x Copper Bar

● 4x Tin Sheet

● 32x Nails

Hard Wood Plank can be obtained by cutting down Hard Wood Trees (they required a Copper Axe).

Most of these items should be familiar except the Iron Bar.

Iron Bar is made from Iron Ore, which can only be obtained once you have unlocked the Deep Mines.

Unlocking The Deep Mines

The Deep Mines is an area that you can explore underneath your Island and obtain lots of rare ores. It is also one of the better places to make Dinks, so its well worth getting it when you can.

There are a few requirements for unlocking The Deep Mines. First, you need to purchase the Deep Mines Licence for 3,500 Permit Points from Fletch.

This will then unlock the Mines Land Deed, which will allow you to build an elevator that will take you down into the Deep Mines.

The Mine Deed will put your Island into 250,000 Dinks Debt and requires the following materials:

- 10x Bag Of Cement

- 10x Old Cog

- 1x Old Contraption

- 2x Old Key

- 5x Tin Ore

- 5x Copper Ore

You can obtain the Old Contraption, Old Key and Old Cog from digging up Metal Barrels with your Metal Detector.

A Bag Of Cement comes from grinding up a stone in Stone Grinder.

Once you have gotten the Materials for the Deep Mine, it will take two days for the construction to be complete.

The Deep Mines

The Deep Mines is an epic place to explore and you will almost for sure get lost on your first visit.

Every time you want to enter the Deep Mines, you need to buy a Mine Pass from John for 25,000 Dinks! It's an expensive trip, so make sure you're well prepared each time you go down there.

You should take plenty of healing food and buy a Torch from John to help navigate.

Each time you enter the Deep Mines the map is hidden and requires you to explore it bit by bit.

In the Deep Mines you can find all sorts of goodies, including the Iron Ore Rocks that you can mine for Iron Bars.

The Town Hall

Iron Ore can only be forged in a Furnace, so you may need to buy one from John if you don't already have one (they cost 30,000 Dinks each).

Once you have all the materials, it'll take two days for the Town

Hall to be completed.

That wraps up part 4 of the Dinkum Walkthrough! A lot of Dinks need to be earned in this part, so let us know in the comments if you have a good money-making method!

GUIDES

CRAFTING GUIDE

Crafting in Dinkum is important to upgrading your Island, weapons and functionality. You'll be crafting right from the beginning of your time on Dinkum, with it getting progressively more complex as the game expands and you find new materials.

You can craft items using a Crafting Table; by default this is found in the Base Tent at the beginning of the game, however you can craft more later.

Crafting In Dinkum requires you to obtain special Recipes. These can come from a number of objectives in the game such as completing tasks or unlocking a new Dinkum Licence.

Crafting items in Dinkum will also increase your Dinkum Milestone.

Use our Crafting Material guide to see where you can find required materials.

Crafting Bench Items in Dinkum

Item	Description	Materials	Requirements
Scythe	3 Attack Power	1x Palm Wood Plank 1x Tin Bar	Acquire the Farming Licence

Copper Axe	3 Attack Power	1x Basic Axe 2x Copper Bar	Acquire the Logging Licence Level 2
Iron Axe	4 Attack Power	1x Copper Axe 2x Iron Bar	Acquire the Logging Licence Level 3
Copper Pickaxe	2 Attack Power	1x Basic Pickaxe 2x Copper Bar	Acquire the Mining Licence Level 2
Iron Pickaxe	3 Attack Power	1x Copper Pickaxe 2x Iron Bar	Acquire the Mining Licence Level 3

Copper Watering Can		1x Watering Can 5x Copper Bar	Acquire the Farming Licence Level 2
Iron Watering Can		1x Copper Watering Can 5x Iron Bar	Acquire the Farming Licence Level 3
Copper Hoe	1 Attack Power	1x Hoe 2x Copper Bar	Acquire the Farming Licence Level 2
Iron Hoe	1 Attack Power	1x Copper Hoe 4x Iron Bar	Acquire the Farming Licence Level 3

Copper Fishing Rod		1x Fishing Rod 2x Copper Bar	Acquire the Farming Licence Level 3
Basic Spear	4 Attack Power Used to attack animals	1x Gum Wood Plank 1x Tin Bar	Acquire the Hunting Licence
Copper Spear	7 Attack Power	1x Palm Wood Plank 2x Copper Bar	Obtained from Hunting Licence Level 2
Iron Spear	10 Attack Power	1x Palm Wood Plank 2x Iron Bar	Obtained from Hunting Licence Level 3

Wooden Bat	3 Attack Power Used to attack animals	1x Gum Wood Plank 2x Spinifex Resin	Acquire the Hunting Licence
Croc Teeth Bat	6 Attack Power	1x Copper Bar 2x Spinifex Resin 2x Crocodile Teeth 2x Hardwood Plank	Obtained from Hunting Licence Level 2
Flaming Bat	8 Attack Power	1x Iron Bar 2x Spinifex Resin 2x Flame Sac 2x Hard Wood Plank	Obtained from Hunting Licence Level 3
Basic Hammer	8 Attack Power Used to attack animals	1x Gum Wood Plank 3x Tin Bar	Acquire the Hunting Licence
	13 Attack	1x Gum Wood	Obtained from Hunting Licence

Copper Hammer	Power	Plank 3x Copper Bar	Level 2
Iron Hammer	18 Attack Power	2x Hard Wood Plank 3x Iron Bar	Obtained from Hunting Licence Level 3
Animal Trap		1x Iron Bar 1x Hard Wood Plank 2x Old Spring	Obtained from Trapping Licence
Simple Animal Trap		1x Tin Bar 8x Mangrove Stick 1x Old Spring	Obtained from Trapping Licence Level 2

Rock Path	Build a simple rock path	2x Stone	Default
Palm Wood Path		2x Palm Wood Plank	Default
Gum Wood Path		2x Gum Wood Plank	Default
Hard Wood Path		2x Hard Wood Plank	Default

Brick Path		2x Stone	Default
Cement Path		2x Bag Of Cement	Default
Stone Steps		1x Brick Path 1x Bag Of Cement	Default
Palm Wood Steps		1x Palm Wood Path 1x Nails	Default

Crude Fence		2x Gum Log 1x Spinifex Resin	Default
Palm Wood Fence		3x Palm Wood Plank 4x Nails	
Gum Wood Fence		3x Gum Wood Plank 4x Nails	
Hard Wood Fence		3x Hard Wood Plank 4x Nails	

 Brick Fence		2x Stone 1x Bag Of Cement	
 Cement Fence		4x Bag Of Cement	
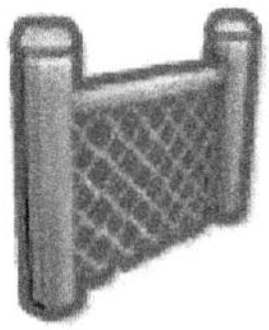 Tin Fence		4x Tin Sheet	
 Hedge		2x Spinifex Tuft 2x Fern Seed 2x Bush Seed	

Iron Cement Fence		1x Bag Of Cement 1x Iron Bar	Obtained from Fletch Daily Task
Palm Wood Gate		2x Palm Wood Plank 4x Nails	
Gum Wood Gate		2x Gum Wood Plank 4x Nails	
Hard Wood Gate		2x Hard Wood Plank 4x Nails	

Tin Gate		2x Tin Sheet	
Hedge Arch		2x Hedge 1x Palm Wood Plank 2x Spinifex Resin	
Palm Wood Bridge		15x Palm Wood Plank 15x Nails	Acquire the Building Licence
Hard Wood Bridge		15x Nails 15x Hard Wood Plank	Acquire the Building Licence

Gum Wood Bridge		15x Nails 15x Gum Wood Plank	Acquire the Building Licence
Brick Bridge		5x Bag Of Cement 15x Stone	Acquire the Building Licence
Brick Fountain		5x Stone 1x Sprinkler 5x Bag Of Cement	Purchasable from Franklyn
Camp Fire	Allows you to cook food	2x Gum Log 3x Stone	Default

Crude Furnace	Turns Ore into Bars	3x Stone 1x Camp Fire 5x Tin Ore	Given by Fletch following the main story
Garden Light		1x Quartz Crystal 2x Tin Sheet 1x Glass Bulb	
Wooden Torch		1x Mangrove Stick	Default
StreetLamp		1x Quartz Crystal 1x Iron Bar 1x Glass Bulb	

Wooden Lamp Post		1x Palm Wood Fence 1x Nails 1x Quartz Crystal 1x Wooden Torch	
Copper Street Lamp		1x Quartz Crystal 1x Copper Bar 1x Glass Bulb	Obtained from Melvin
Mushroom Lamp		15x Glowing Mushroom 2x Quartz Crystal 1x Glass Bulb	
Festoon Lights		2x Gum Wood Plank 4x Bright Wire 3x Glass Bulb	

 Wooden Flower Bed		2x Gum Wood Plank 1x Nails	
 Brick Flower Bed		2x Bag Of Cement 1x Stone	
 Scarecrow		1x Pumpkin 2x Gum Log 8x Spinifex Tuft	
 Compost Bin		8x Hard Wood Plank 3x Copper Bar 1x Tin Sheet 15x Nails	

Sprinkler		5x Copper Bar 4x Quartz Crystal 4x Old Spring 4x Old Gear	
Advanced Sprinkler		1x Sprinkler 5x Iron Bar 4x Old Gear 4x Old Spring 1x Hot Cylinder	
Water Tank		15x Hard Wood Plank 15x Tin Sheet 1x Old Contraption 8x Iron Bar 8x Nails	
		25x Stone 15x Tin Sheet 10x Bag Of Cement	

Silo		8x Quartz Crystal 5x Iron bar	
Spinning Wheel		4x Palm Wood Plank 4x Old Gear 1x Old Wheel	
Cheese Maker			Obtained from Rayne Daily Task
Grain Mill		4x Gum Wood Plank 1x Old Gear 2x Copper Bar 1x Old Wheel	Acquire the Farming Licence
Cooking Table		5x Palm Wood Plank 2x Nails 1x Tin Bar	Default

		1x Tin Sheet	
Crafting Table	Allows you to craft any of these items in this table.	3x Gum Wood Plank 1x Tin Bar 3x Nails	Default
Wooden Crate	Allows you to store items inside	1x Palm Wood Plank 2x Gum Wood Plank 1x Nails	Given by Fletch following the main story
Bird Coop		4x Copper Bar 4x Spinifex Turf 2x Tin Sheet 3x Gum Wood Plank 4x Nails	Obtained from Handling Licence
Animal Stall		3x Iron Bar 2x Spinifex Tuft 8x Hard Wood Plank 2x Tin Sheet	

		8x Nails	
Animal Den		3x Bag Of Cement 4x Stone 1x Copper Bar	
Keg		5x Palm Wood Plank 1x Iron Bar	Acquire the Logging Licence Level 2
Animal Collection Point		2x Palm Wood Plank 2x Hard Wood Plank 1x Nails	
Windmill		20x Tin Sheet 5x Old Gear 5x Old Spring 5x Iron Bar	

		2x Old Wheel	
Palm Wood Bench		5x Palm Wood Plank 4x Nails	Obtained from Sally's Daily Task
Nails (8)		1x Tin Bar	Given by Fletch following the main story
Row Boat	Allows you to row across water	10x Gum Wood Plank 10x Palm Wood Plank 2x Tin Bar 4x Nails	Obtained from the Vehicle Licence

Cooking Table Items Dinkum

The Cooking Table can be crafted at the Crafting Table. The Cooking Table allows you to craft various foods that give stats.

Item	Description	Materials	Buffs

Meat Stick	+35 Health +15 Energy	3x Meat 1x Mangrove Stick	Defence Buff for 3 minutes
Dagwood Dog	+15 Max Health +25 Max Energy	1x Corn 1x Meat 1x Mangrove Stick	Attack Buff for 3 minutes Defence Buff for 3 minutes
Bread	+35 Health +25 Energy	3x Flour	Advanced Defence Buff for 3 minutes
Fairy Bread	+10 Energy	1x Bread 2x Sugar	Speed Buff for 2 minutes

Damper	+25 Max Health +15 Max Energy	1x Flour 1x Milk	Advanced Mining Buff for 5 minutes
Meat Pie	+25 Max Health +5 Max Energy	1x Flour 1x Meat 1x Raw Drumstick	Advanced Attack Buff for 3 minutes
Pastie	+30 Max Health +30 Max Energy	1x Flour 1x Cabbage 1x Carrot 1x Potato	Super Advanced Mining Buff for 5 minutes Super Advanced Logging Buff for 5 minutes
Quiche	+20 Max Health +30 Max Energy	1x Flour 1x Chicken Egg 1x Cheese	Super Advanced Mining Buff for 5 minutes Super Advanced Logging Buff for 5 minutes Speed Buff for 5

			minutes
Sausage Roll	+30 Max Health +30 Max Energy	1x Flour 1x Chicken Egg 1x Meat 1x Onion	Advanced Attack Buff for 5 minutes Advanced Defence Buff for 5 minutes Speed Buff for 5 minutes
Fruit Salad	+10 Health +20 Energy	2x Bush Lime 2x Apple 2x Banana 2x Quandong	Logging Buff for 5 Minutes Defence Buff for 5 minutes
Fish and Chips	+10 Max Health +30 Max Energy	1x Flake 2x Potato 1x Bush Lime	Super Advanced Fishing Buff for 20 minutes
	+45 Max Health +10 Max Energy	1x Meat 1x Potato 1x Onion 1x Carrot	Attack Buff for 3 minutes Advanced Defence Buff for 3 minutes

Hearty Stew			
Prime Roast	+50 Max Health +50 Max Energy	1x Raw Prime Meat 3x Potato 2x Carrot 1x Kale 3x Green Bean 1x Pumpkin	Super Advanced Attack Buff for 5 minutes Super Advanced Defence Buff for 5 minutes
Lamington	+30 Health +30 Energy	1x Flour 1x Sugar 1x Coconut 1x Chicken Egg 1x Milk	Advanced Mining Buff for 4 minutes Advanced Logging Buff for 4 minutes Advanced Defence Buff for 4 minutes Super Advanced Speed Buff for 59 seconds
Pavlova	+45 Max Health +45 Max Energy	4x Big Chicken Egg 2x Sugar 1x Fruit Salad	Super Advanced Unknown for 3 minutes Advanced Hunting Buff for 10 minutes

MINING GUIDE

Mining in Dinkum is one of the core professions that allow you to gather crafting materials to progress your Island. It is one of the first tools you learn to use and this guide will go over everything to do with Mining In Dinkum.

- Mining Tools

- Dinkum Ore Types

- Ruby and Amber Chunk

- Best place to find Bronze Ore, Iron Ore and Tin Ore

Every time you use a Pickaxe to mine ore in Dinkum, it raises your Mining Level. Increasing your Mining Level will allow you to purchase Mining Licences that upgrade your Mining Tools.

There are several types of Ore you can find in Dinkum and they can be used to craft better tools, weapons and upgrade your Island buildings.

There are three Mining Licences you can acquire

- Level 1 - 250 Permit Points

- Level 2 - 1,000 Permit Points (Level 10 Mining)

- Level 3 - 3,000 Permit Points (Level 20 Mining)

Mining Tools

There are several Mining Tools you can acquire in Dinkum to help you mine precious ores. Below are all the Mining Tools you need and how to get them.

Tool	Requirements	Obtained From
Pickaxe	Mining Licence Level 1	John's Goods Store
Copper Pickaxe	Mining Licence Level 2 Level 10 Mining	Crafting Table
Iron Pickaxe	Mining Licence Level 3 Level 20 Mining	Crafting Table

Jack Hammer	Mining Licence Level 3 Level 20 Mining	Franklyn's Crafting Laboratory

Dinkum Ore Types

There are several types of Ore you can mine in Dinkum. Some of them can be used for crafting and others can be sold for lots of Dinks. Below is a list of Ore you can find.

Ore Type	Converts To	Obtained From	Tool	Sells For
Stone	Bag Of Cement	Rock	Stone Grinder	10 Dinks
Tin Ore	Tin Bar	Tin Rock	Crude Furnace / Furnace	25 Dinks

			Crude Furnace / Furnace	50 Dinks
 Copper Ore	 Copper Bar	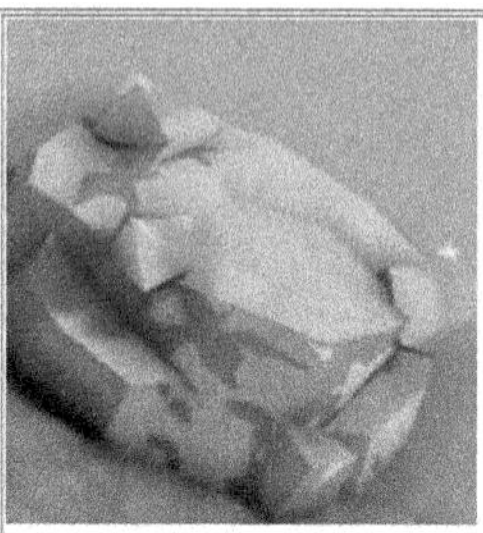 Copper Rock		
 Iron Ore	 Iron Bar	 Iron Rock	Furnace	100 Dinks
 Quartz Crystal	N/A	 Quartz Rock	–	200 Dinks
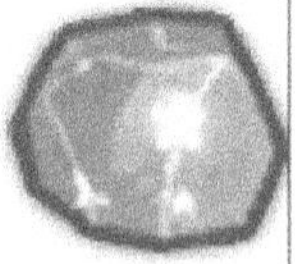 Shiny Stone	 Tin Ore	Any Rock	Stone Grinder	100 Dinks

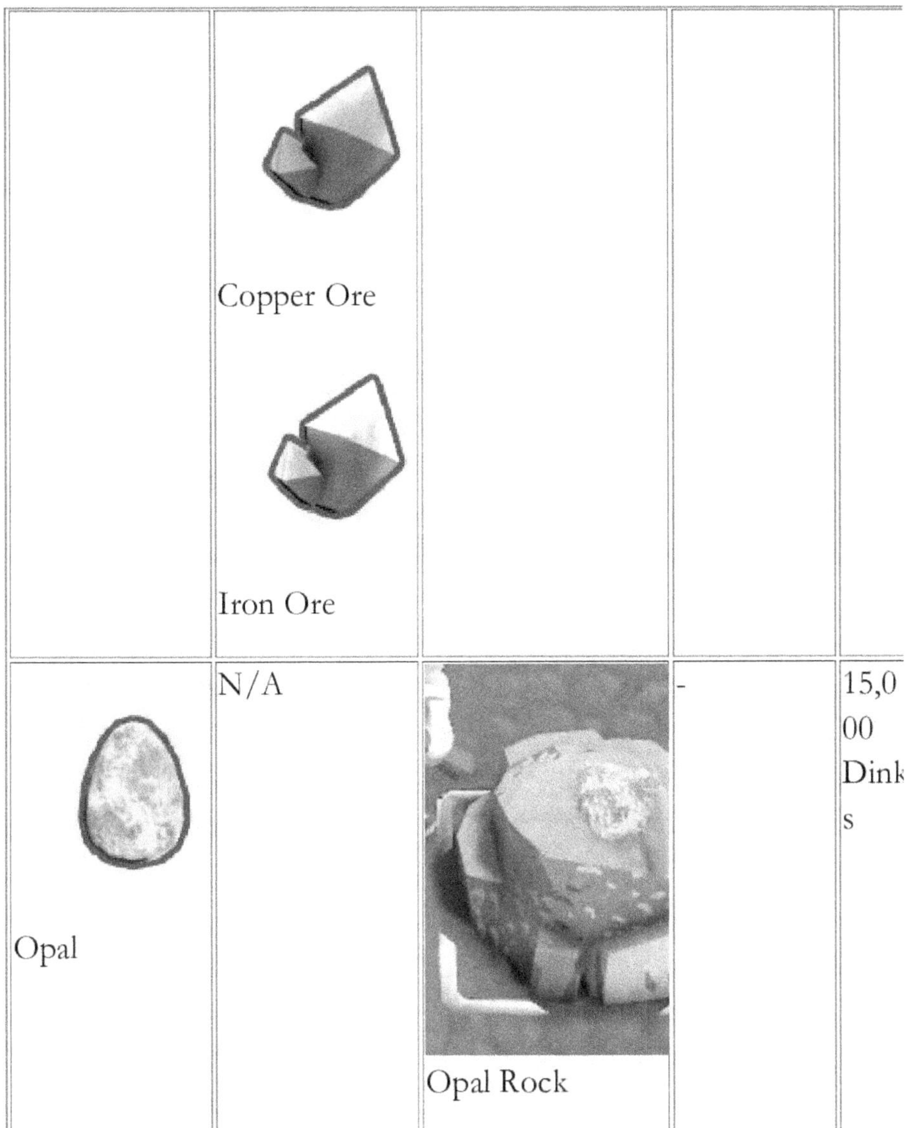

Copper Ore

Iron Ore

Opal

N/A

Opal Rock

-

15,0
00
Dink
s

Ruby and Amber Chunk

There are two special types of rare ore/gems that you can also find; these ore do not go into your Inventory- instead you have to carry them!

Amber Chunk can be found around your Island buried in the ground. When you dig it up with a Shovel, you can carry it on your head or use a vehicle to transport it.

Ruby can be found in the Deep Mines; you'll need to use your Pickaxe to break it out and then carry it back to the Elevator.

Both of these ores can be sold to John for Dinks. You place them on the scale in his shop and he will pay between 30,000-90,000 Dinks depending on the weight of the ore.

Best place to find Bronze Ore, Iron Ore and Tin Ore

When you first start your Island, you'll find plenty of Tin Ore, Bronze Ore and Quartz Ore Rocks all around your Island. The rocks will regenerate over time, so if you're struggling to find a specific type of Ore, just let a few days go by and you should see some pop up.

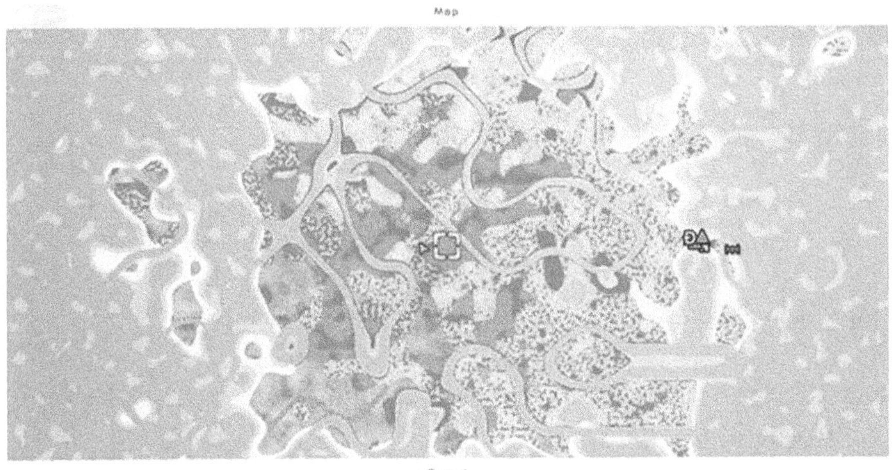

Some of the best areas to find Tin Ore, Bronze Ore and Quartz Ore are Desert Areas. There are usually huge clusters of rocks to break up and if you check your world map you can find Desert Areas by hovering over the orange spots.

However, the best spot for gathering ore materials is The Deep Mine. There are quite a few requirements to access this place, but it is well worth it. It will also cost you 25,000 Dinks each time you head to the Deep Mines but you can easily make this back by finding Rubys and selling them to John.

Once there, you can mine until you run out of energy. It is the most reliable way to get all Ore types.

Once you unlock The Deep Mines, you will also start to find Iron Ore Rocks all over your Island, as well as Opal Ore Rocks. Opals sell for 15,000 Dinks each!

FISHING GUIDE

Fishing is one of the main skills you can upgrade in Dinkum and this guide will give you all the details you need on how to catch all the Fish in Dinkum, the best fishing tools and other fishing tips and tricks.

- How To Fish in Dinkum

- Fishing Tools

To Fish in Dinkum you need a Fishing Rod and the basic Fishing Licence from Fletch.

How To Fish in Dinkum

Fishing is relatively easy in Dinkum and all it requires is the Fishing Rod tool. You can fish in any area on your Island where there is water. You can usually see all the Fish in the water that you might be able to catch, so you don't need to do too much waiting around to get a nibble.

When you see a Fish, cast your Fishing Rod. You can hold down the casting action button for a longer cast.

Fish will then head towards your Fishing Rod's Hook. The fish will then nibble on your hook, and you'll hear several splashing sounds.

You'll only want to start reeling when you hear a large splash sound and the Fishing Rod's Bobber sinks deeper into the water. When you see this animation, start reeling in the Fish.

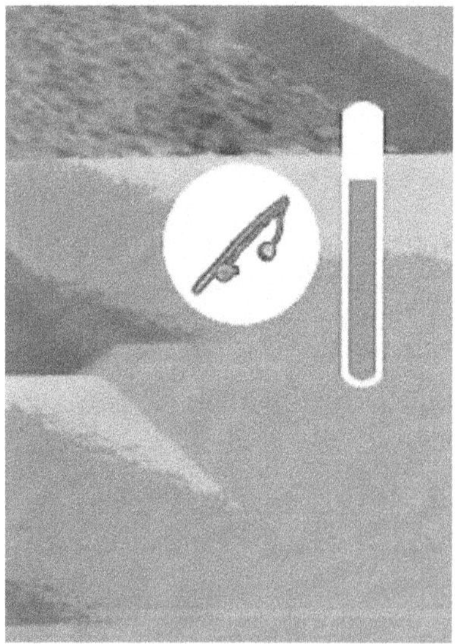

Your Fishing Rod will have a Reel Meter on the side of it. If you hold down the Reel button as the Fish is swimming away, it will use up it's power. If the power reaches zero, the Fish will break free and get away.

One tip for is to spam-click the Reel button rather than hold it down.

This will reel the fish in but not use up your Reel Power.

The different types of Fishing Tools will give you more power and faster ability to reel the Fish in.

When you catch a Fish, it goes into your Inventory taking up one slot. It does not stack, so you can easily fill up your Inventory quite fast.

You can either sell Fish for Dinks or store them in your Museum.

Fishing Tools

There are a few Fishing Tools you can use to catch Fish. Each Fishing tool will allow you to catch rarer fish that require more power to reel them in, so it's always best to upgrade your Fishing Rod when you can.

Tool	Requirements	Obtained From
Fishing Rod	Fishing Licence Level 1	John's Goods Store
Copper Fishing Rod	Fishing Licence Level 2 Fishing Level 5	Crafting Table

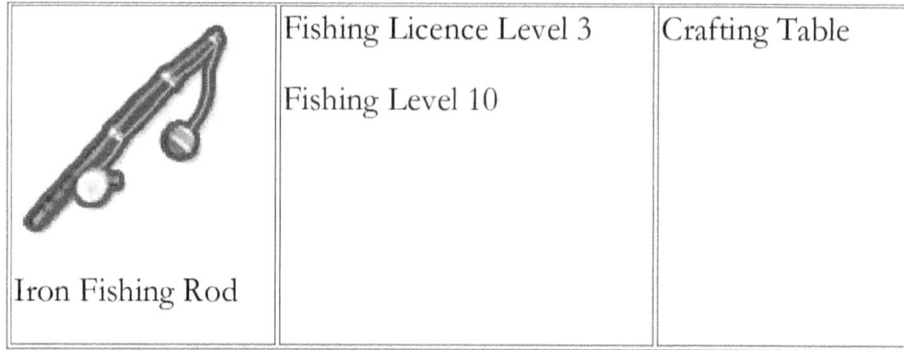 Iron Fishing Rod	Fishing Licence Level 3 Fishing Level 10	Crafting Table

You might also want to consider crafting a Rowing Boat or Jetskii from Franklyn so that you can go further out into the deeper parts of the ocean.

FARMING GUIDE

Farming in Dinkum is a great way to earn money and this guide will go over all aspects of farming, including how to make millions of dinks, all the farming tools and all the items you can grow.

- How To Plant Seeds In Dinkum

- Advanced Dinkum Farming - Sprinklers And Water Tanks

To begin Farming in Dinkum, you first need to purchase a Farming Licence from Fletch.

How To Plant Seeds In Dinkum

To create your own farm, you'll need these basic items:

A Hoe Tool

A Watering Can

Some Seeds

Farming Licence

All of these can be purchased from Rayne.

Once you have a Hoe, you start by plowing the ground to make it fertile to plant seeds. You can create a massive stretch of land to plant, or just a small little garden. It's up to you!

Then you need to plant your seeds. Select them from your Toolbelt and they will be planted in the fertile squares. All seeds start off in their basic stage and will grow as each day passes.

You will need to water your plants each day. On some days, it rains on your Island and you won't have to water them that day. If you don't water them, the plants won't progress.

As a beginner farmer, you'll be able to purchase a Watering Can. You can fill up your Watering Can in shallow water anywhere on your island, so it's a good idea to keep your farm close to water so you don't have to travel too far. Better yet, you can craft a Water Tank/Fountain and use that to fill up your Watering Can.

Each seed type has it's own time-duration of how many days it takes to fully grow. Some seeds only grow in certain seasons and others grow all year round.

When it's time to harvest, you can either use an Axe to chop them down, or craft a Scythe, which has a wider range for collecting your crops.

You can decide what you'd like to do next; you can either sell your Harvest as it is, or you can use the ingredients to craft other food using various machines. Take a look at the Cooking Table for the different recipes.

Advanced Dinkum Farming - Sprinklers And Water Tanks

Starting off at level 1 farming in Dinkum is very slow. The tools let you plant seeds one by one and it takes forever if you're trying to create a giant field of crops.

Luckily, as you level up, better tools become available and make the whole farming process that much easier. In fact, a lot of it becomes automated and all you need to do is harvest the crops and sell them for big dink!

Your first target should be to level up your Farming skill to level 10 and then level 20. This will allow you to unlock the Farming Licences Level 2 and 3, which in turn grant new tools for harvesting.

You can level up farming by planting seeds, using your Hoe Tool to soften the ground, harvesting your crops and make food out of any harvested crops.

Level 3 Farming will then unlock Irrigation Licence, which allows you to craft Sprinklers! These will automatically water your crops for you- if you get to Level 2 Irrigation you unlock the Advanced Sprinkler that can water even more crops.

The final piece of the puzzle for farming is the Tractor. This expensive machine can be crafted by Franklyn, but it costs 1,500,000 Dinks! The Tractor is a vehicle you can drive that has 3 tools attached to it (they are unlocked based on your Arigcultural Vehicle Licence) that allow you to farm huge areas very fast.

If you want to speed up how fast your crops grow, you can also plant Fertilizer on your soil just before you put down your seeds.

When it comes to making money, one of the easiest methods is to plant Wheat Seeds, harvest it and turn it into flour and then make Bread at the Cooking Table; Bread sells at 6,000 Dinks each. You can also sell it for 50% more to Jimmy.

THE DEEP MINES

The Deep Mines is an area in Dinkum that you can access to find lots of rare ores, Iron Ore and make plenty of money/dinks. This guide will give an overview of what you can find in the Deep Mines, how to unlock it and other tips and tricks!

- How To Unlock The Deep Mines

- Surviving The Deep Mines

- What can you find in the Deep Mines

- How To Unlock The Deep Mines

In order to access the Deep Mines, you first need to have Level 2 Mining Licence.

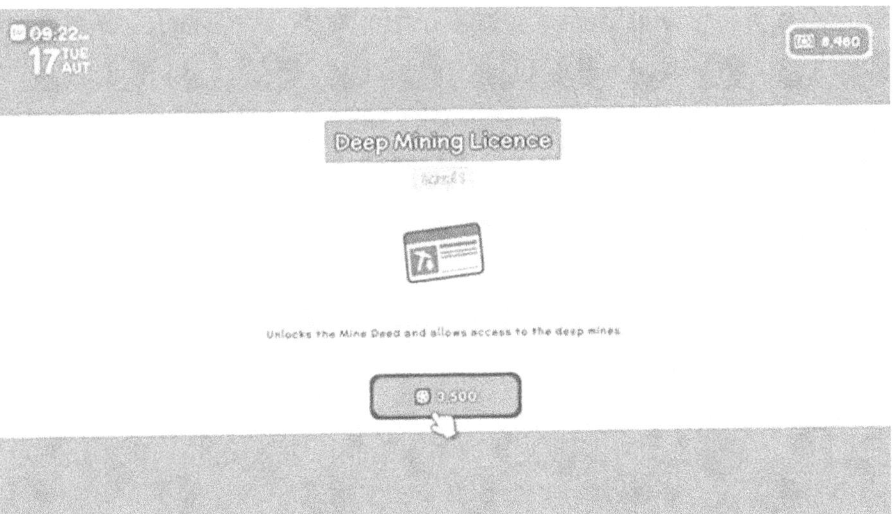

This will then unlock the Deep Mining Licence that you can purchase for 3,500 Permit Points. This will then unlock the Mine Deed that you can apply for from Fletch.

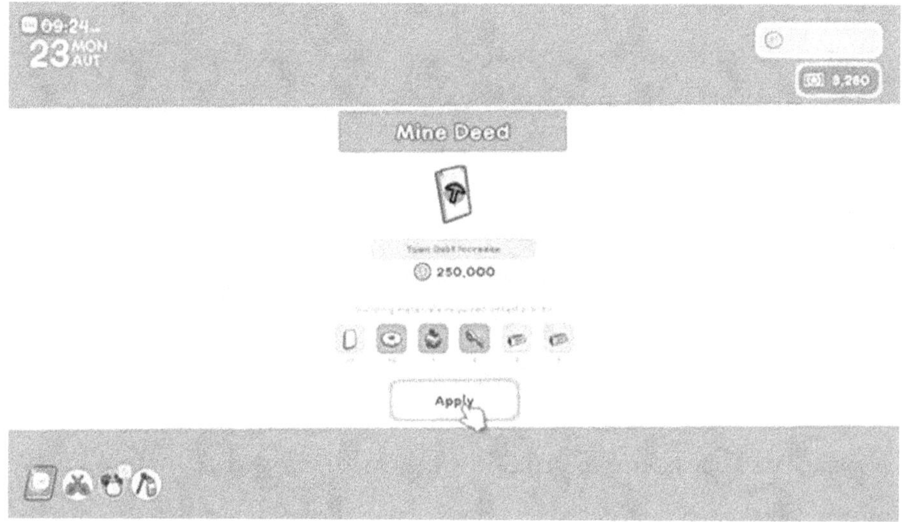

The Mine Deed will put your Island into 250,000 Dinks Debt and requires the following materials:

- 10x Bag Of Cement

- 10x Old Cog

- 1x Old Contraption

- 2x Old Key

- 5x Tin Ore

- 5x Copper Ore

Once you have constructed the Mine Elevator, you will then need to purchase a Mine Pass from John's Goods, which costs 25,000 Dinks.

This pass is a one-time-use, so you will need to purchase another one each time you head into the mines.

Surviving The Deep Mines

The Deep Mines is a huge labyrinth that has very little lighting and lots of enemies hidden around. Each time you arrive in the Deep Mines, your map is completely obscured and reset every time you leave.

You'll find plenty of enemies here and so you'll want to maximize your health and stamina bars. You can eat certain fruits and meats to increase your bars; the best is Cooked Crocodile Meat as this will increase your health by +25 and stamina by +10.

You'll also want to make sure your carry a Torch, which can be purchased from John for 6,000 Dinks. When active, this will light up your immediate surroundings and is vital to getting around The Deep Mines.

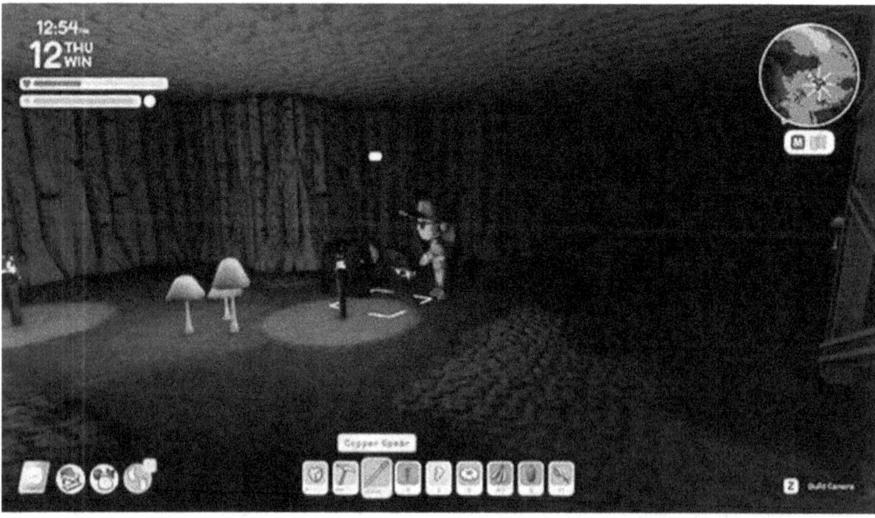

When fighting, you'll obviously want some strong weapons. At a minimum you want Copper strength weapons, but if you've unlocked them, the Iron Spear and Flaming Bat are great.

It is also a good idea to take some Wooden Torch's with you and place them on the ground when you get ambushed to help you see better.

You will come across Bats very often in the Deep Mines and they are very annoying. They will follow you for a long time and are hard to hit; luckily one swipe from a normal Spear should be enough to take them out. If you have unlocked the Flaming Bat, this weapon is great at taking them out as you can jump and hit them as they are flying around you.

If you die in the Deep Mines, you will return to the Elevator Shaft where you can heal up and go again (or return back to the surface).

You cannot sleep in the Deep Mines or the Elevator with your Sleeping Bag. You also cannot drop loot inside the Elevator apart from rare Gemstones.

What can you find in the Deep Mines

The Deep Mine is host to lots of treasure that can make you RICH in Dinkum. The cost of going down into the mines in 25K, but you should be able to make that back and more after each visit.

The Glowing Mushrooms are not worth much so it's best to leave them in place for extra light.

Keep an eye out for old rusty cars; these are like Metal Barrels and can drop lots and lots of materials when you destroy them with your Pickaxe. You can also find Bins buried in the ground that also give you the same loot.

You'll also find plenty of Tin, Copper and Iron Ore down here, so make sure you bring your Iron Pickaxe for farming. This is the best area in the game for mining.

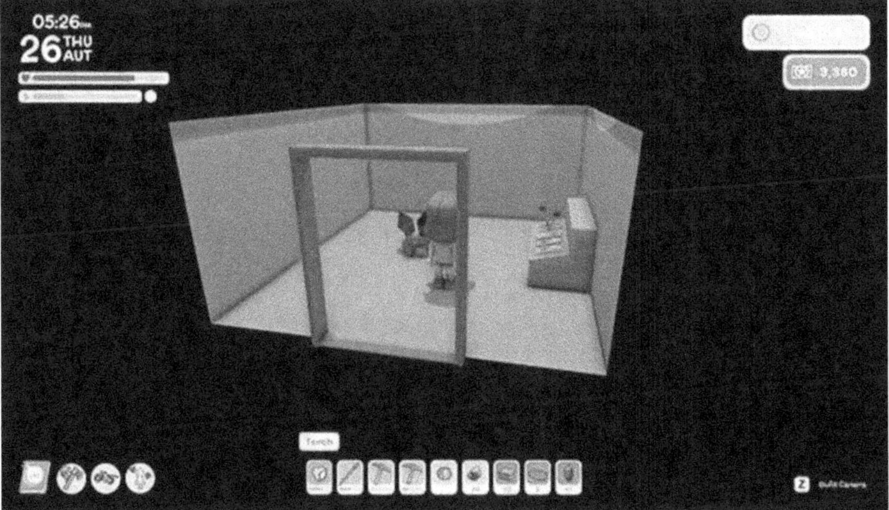

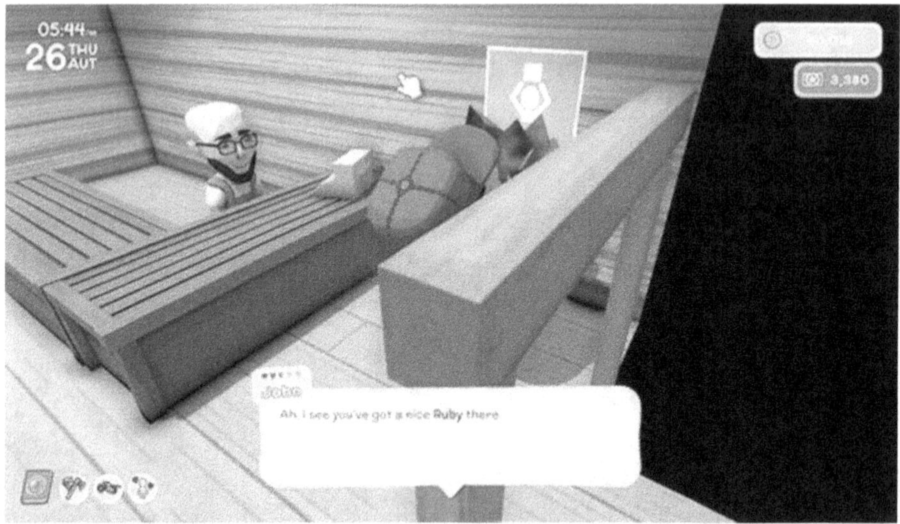

You might also come across Rubys, which are hidden inside rocks. You will have to carry these to the Elevator Shaft and place them there until you're ready to go back up.

You can sell Rubys to John by placing them on the scales in his shop. You can earn anywhere from 30,000-80,0000 Dinks per Ruby!

Deep Mine Treasure Chests

Each time you enter the Deep Mines, the map is completely remade.

And every time it is remade, there are several stone temples put in that you can unlock using an Old Key.

Old Key can be found from Metal Barrels, Metal Cars and Dustbins. You need two Old Keys to enter a Stone Temple.

Inside a Stone Temple, you'll find a single Treasure Chest. These Treasure Chests hold all sorts of items. Check out the table below for a list.

Item	Type
Iron Bar	Crafting Material
Copper Bar	Crafting Material
Fertilizer	Farming Material
Copper Spear	Weapon
Iron Hammer	Weapon

Flaming Bat	Weapon
Slingshot	Weapon
Guitar	Musical Instrument
Paint	Decorative Item
Circuit Board	Crafting Material
Old Contraption	Crafting Material
Opal	Rare Gem
Boogie Board	Swimming

HOW TO MAKE MONEY

This guide will teach you how to make money in Dinkum using some easy techniques that can be used at the beginning of the game, middle game and end-game.

- Cooking Meat
- Farming Fruit - Orchard Method
- Farming Bread Method

In Dinkum having lots of Dinks will make your life easier when it comes to purchasing the best tools, vehicles and items in the game.

Every item you farm can be sold to NPC John and there are various items in the game that are worth more than others. This guide will look at the best techniques that allow you to make millions of Dinks.

You can also purchase a special Commerce Licence that gives you 5%,10% and 15% extra Dinks when selling them.

If you have a method that you'd like to share, use the comment section below this post.

Cooking Meat

One of the best methods in Dinkum to make money is to hunt the animals on your Island for Meat. An animal can drop up to 3 pieces of Meat at a time and there is an unlimited resource of them.

Most enemies can be killed with just the basic weapons, so this method is decent for early game. We recommend using the Spear weapon, as it is fast and allows you to attack from range.

As you hunt for meat, you'll learn you can easily dodge most enemy attacks by waiting for the right moment. Some enemies also get "stunned", allowing you to get several hits in.

Once you have your Meat, you'll want to cook it. This will increase the price you can sell it for, so it's well worth taking the time to do so. If you craft 10 or so campfires, that means you can cook 10 pieces of Meat at a time and they take less than 20 seconds to cook fully.

Once you have a healthy stack, go and sell them to John.

Note: Hunting Crocodile will also yield Crocodile Tooth, which sell for 3,650 Dinks each!

Below is a table of meat in the game and their prices.

Item	Sells For	Sells For Cooked	Dropped By
Meat	400 Dinks	800 Dinks	Kangaroo, Wolves, Hedgehog, Boars
Croco Meat	625 Dinks	1,750 Dinks	Crocodile
Raw Drumstick	350 Dinks	700 Dinks	Chickens
Giant Raw	500 Dinks	1,500 Dinks	Dodo Birds

Drumstick			
Flake	950 Dinks	1,900 Dinks	Shark

Farming Fruit - Orchard Method

Probably one of the most broken ways in Dinkum to make money is to create your own Orchard by planting fruit. This can be done at any stage of the game, including right at the beginning, and you can make millions of Dinks depending on how far you want to go.

Planting a fruit will cause it to grow into a tree, where it will then bear more Fruit that you can harvest. You don't have to water them and they will constantly keep bearing new fruit over a week-long period. All you need to do is spam next day and you'll have more fruit to pick.

The plan then, is to bury hundreds of fruits so they grow into hundreds of trees. You'll then get hundreds, if not thousands, of fruits every week or so. Sell them all to John and you can easily rack up a million Dinks.

There are some tools you can use to help you with this method. First, you'll obviously need a Shovel to bury the Fruit. You'll need to dig a hole, drop a single fruit into the hole, and then cover it with soil. Your Shovel can carry the soil it's dug, so you can rebury it with the same soil you dig out, making it super fast to plant trees.

If you want to make a huge Orchard, considering buying Axes cut down trees and your Pickaxe for taking out rocks.

You can also buy the Compactor for leveling the ground from Franklyn. This will make your ground a lot smoother and a lot easier to plant trees.

There are several types of Fruit in Dinkum you can plant, but the best type of fruit to plant is a Banana. It drops in bunches of 2 and sells for 248 Dinks each. Other fruits may drop more, but they sell for way less than the Banana.

Check out our Orchard of Bananas below; every week this nets 100K Dinks. It takes a couple of hours to get the setup, but once done, you'll have a never-ending supply of Dinks!

Farming Bread Method

Bread is one of the best items to sell as it goes for 6,300 Dinks each and all it requires is 3 Flour items to craft.

This method requires a bit of a setup in order to get it produce you enough Bread with little effort, but once it is setup, you can continue to reap the benefits after. There is a video below of us earning over 3,500,000 Dinks in one session!

Whilst you can do this method with just the basic tools, it's a lot more productive to have the following requirements:

Farming Licence Level 3

Irrigation Licence Level 2

Agriculture Vehicle Licence Level 3

We'll break down each part of making bread below.

Step 1 - Plant Wheat

You can buy Wheat Seeds from Rayne and they can be planted any time of the year. They'll take around 9 days to fully grow and you'll have to harvest them once ready.

In order for a seed to grow, it needs to have been watered. Some days it will rain and automatically water your plants. However, a better method is to unlock the Irrigation Licence Level 2 and craft Advanced Sprinklers to automatically water your seeds for you all the time.

To get Irrigation Licence, you need to reach level 20 in Farming and purchase the Farming Licence Level 3.

You can then build out a field of crops that is automatically watered for you.

Step 2 - Turn Wheat Into Flour,

Once you harvest your Wheat, you can then turn it into Flour using a Grain Mill. You'll want to craft 10 or so of these so that you can quickly turn your Wheat into Flower. The more Grain Mills the better- you can also build a Windmill to speed up production or just start the next day for instant production.

Once you have your Flour, head to a Cooking Table and craft Bread. This can be a bit tedious as you can only craft 1 bread at a time and this method requires 50 Bread minimum.

Step 3 - Sell Bread To Jimmy

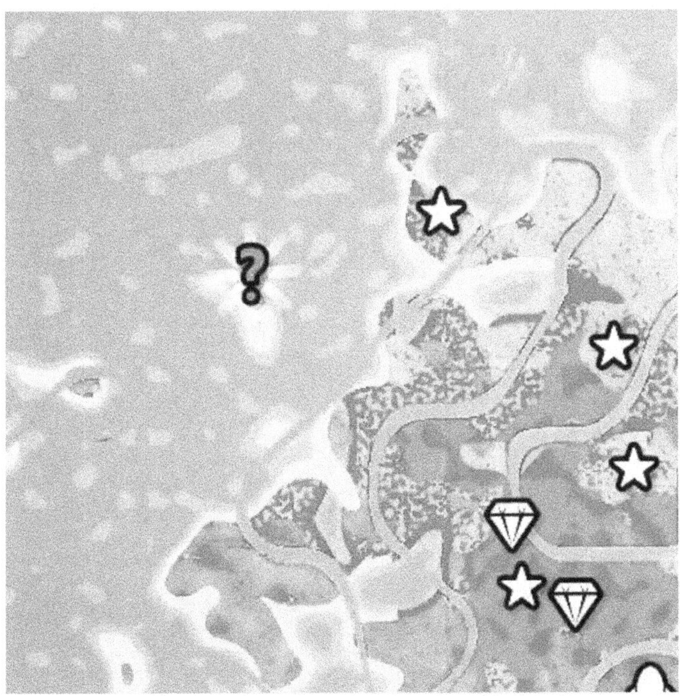

Jimmy is a special NPC that visits your Island when it rains. You must have 1,000,000 Dinks in your Bank also.

On rainy day, check your map and you'll see a special ? icon, which is where Jimmy is located.

Jimmy will buy your items off you for 50% more than John will but he requires you to have at least 50 of the item.

Sell your bread to him in bulk and reap the rewards!

ABOUT THE AUTHOR

When I finding new tricks, tips, and strategies to beat each other, I came up with a brilliant idea. Let's take these hours of gaming expertise, and share these skills with like mind people. At that moment, the Dinkum Complete Guide were born.
Thank you for trusting and choosing this book.